Disney's Year Book

1995

Disney's Year Book 1995

GROLIER ENTERPRISES INC.
Danbury, Connecticut

FERN L. MAMBERG   *Executive Editor*
ELIZABETH A. FARRINGTON   *Art Director*
HARRIETT GREYSTONE   *Production Manager*

ISBN: 0-7172-8449-2
ISSN: 0273-1274

Illustration Credits and Acknowledgments

6—© Fourmay/SABA; 7–9—© Raphael Gaillarde/Gamma-Liaison; 10—Bassignac/Deville/Gaillarde/Gamma-Liaison; 11—Coquelles/Sygma; 12—© Ron Kimball; 13—© Tim Davis/Photo Researchers, Inc.; Ralph A. Geinhold/Animals Animals; © Ariel Skelley/The Stock Market; 14–15—© Richard Orr; 28—Courtesy Fernbank Museum of Natural History, Atlanta, Georgia; Courtesy USDA Forest Service; 29—Courtesy USDA Forest Service; 30—© David Scharf/Peter Arnold, Inc.; 31—© Dr. Jeremy Burgess/Science Photo Library/Photo Researchers, Inc.; Science Photo Library/Photo Researchers, Inc.; 32—© Dr. Jeremy Burgess/Science Photo Library/Photo Researchers, Inc.; © David M. Phillips/Photo Researchers, Inc.; 33—© A.B. Dowsett/Science Photo Library/Photo Researchers, Inc.; © Dr. Jeremy Burgess/Science Photo Library/Photo Researchers, Inc.; 34–35—Designed and created by Jenny Tesar; 48—© Gail Shumway; © Zig Leszczynski/Animals Animals; 49—© Zig Leszczynski/Animals Animals; © Breck P. Kent; © Jany Sauvanet/Photo Researchers, Inc.; 51—© Jane Burton/Bruce Coleman, Inc.; © Gail Shumway; 52—© Michael Fogden; 53—Artist, James Marsh; 54—© Drew Endicott; 55—© Lawrence Migdale; 56–57—Reprinted from OWL Magazine with permission of the Young Naturalist Foundation; 70–71—Artist, Vince Caputo; 72—Artist, Natasha Lessnik; © sv/ho-NASA Reuters/Bettmann; 73—Dr. Christopher Burrows, ESA/STSci and NASA; 131—© Space Telescope Science Institute; 74—AP/Wide World; 77—Designed by Elizabeth A. Farrington; 90—© Andrew J. Martinez; © Jack Reid/Tom Stack & Associates; 91—© Andrew J. Martinez; 92—© Reuters/Bettmann; © Shaun Botterill/Allsport; 93—Reprinted by permission: Tribune Media Services; 94—© Reuters/Bettmann; 95—© Steve Powell/Allsport; © Clive Brunskill

Contents

*A high-speed train enters the Chunnel, an underwater rail tunnel
that runs beneath the English Channel from England to France.*

AN ISLAND NO LONGER

Just before 3:00 P.M. on May 6, 1994, a special train pulled into
Folkestone terminal in south east England. On board was a shiny,
black Rolls Royce carrying two important passengers: Queen
Elizabeth II of Britain and President François Mitterrand of
France. The two heads of state had just completed an historic
journey: They had travelled from France beneath the English
Channel to open the Channel Tunnel officially. Two hundred years
after the first plans were put forward, and after nearly seven years

6

of work, Britain and France were joined by a tunnel—the first time since the Ice Age that the countries have been linked.

The Channel Tunnel—or Chunnel, as it has been nicknamed—is the longest underwater tunnel in the world. It runs from Folkestone to Calais, France. High-speed trains, whipping along at speeds of 100 miles per hour, can make the 31-mile trip in about 35 minutes. And

The Chunnel consists of three tunnels: two tunnels for rail traffic, and a narrower tunnel for service and emergency use.

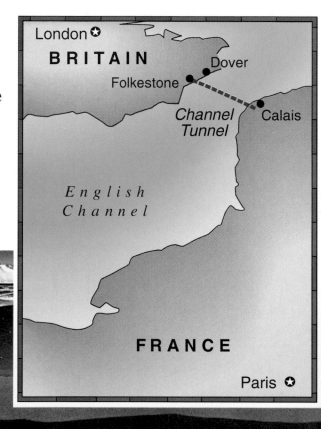

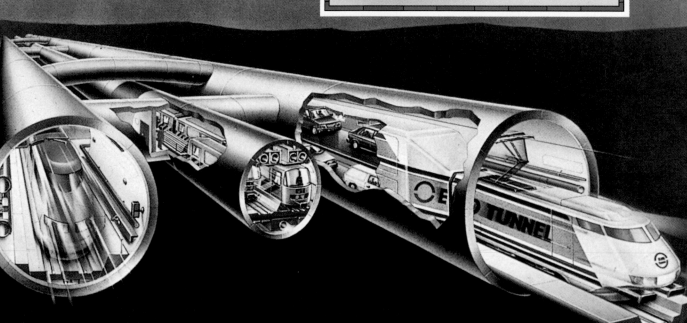

The machines that bored out the Chunnel were bigger than dinosaurs.

unlike the ships that cross the Channel, these trains never have to deal with rough seas and bad weather.

The English Channel is nearly 21 miles across at its narrowest point. Britain's closeness to the continent has allowed it to trade easily with other European countries. But when necessary, Britain could stay apart from the continent—it could gain protection from being an island.

The writer William Shakespeare called Britain "a precious stone set in the silver sea," with the sea protecting the country much like a moat protects a castle. The Channel has been Britain's moat, providing a natural defense for the country. Invaders had to get across the Channel first, and only a few—the Romans and

Normans—succeeded. Others shared the fate of the Spanish Armada, a huge fleet of ships sent to conquer England in 1588; storms scattered the fleet, and many of the ships were lost. The Channel also served as a block to advancing armies in World War I and World War II.

Over the years, many proposals had been put forth to build a tunnel under the Channel. But British military leaders had argued that a tunnel would weaken the security of the country. It was only in the 1980's that politicians finally agreed that conditions were right. A group of French and British companies were given government approval to begin the project.

Work on the Chunnel began in 1987. The design called for two

A Chunnel worker peers into the service and emergency tunnel.

tunnels for rail traffic and a third for service and emergency use. Huge boring machines guided by lasers burrowed through the layers of chalk more than 100 feet below the bottom of the Channel. The drilling teams met midway beneath the Channel in 1990, but work was far from done. The tunnels were then lined with prefabricated concrete. Rail lines and terminals were built, and safety features were added. In all, it took more than 15,000 men to dig the tunnels, at a cost of ten billion pounds!

The tunnel opened in May 1994. Freight began to rumble through the tunnel soon after the opening, and passenger service started in November. Eventually, some fourteen million travellers a year are expected to use the Chunnel. They can drive their cars onto a special train called *Le Shuttle*, ride through the tunnel, and

British and French workers cheer the 1990 Chunnel breakthrough.

Queen Elizabeth and French President Mitterrand complete an historic journey—and the Channel Tunnel is officially opened.

then drive off on the other side. This is much faster than bringing a car across the Channel by ferry boat, which takes about one and a half hours in good weather. Travellers can also board a high-speed passenger train, the *Eurostar*, that can whisk them between London and Paris in three hours, or between London and Brussels, Belgium, in just fifteen minutes more.

The Channel Tunnel has been hailed as one of the most important engineering feats of the 20th century. But it is more than that. It is a symbol of a new chapter in the history of Britain and France, for it is bringing these two nations closer together.

YEAR OF THE DOG

In the Chinese lunar calendar, each year is known by one of twelve animals that make up the Chinese zodiac—and 1994 was the Year of the Dog. That made it an especially good time to take note of dogs and the roles they play in our lives. Dogs have shared our lives for thousands of years, ever since their ancestors gave up their wild ways and began to live with us.

Dogs have adapted to our way of life. Still, many of their tame traits are really "echoes" of their old and long-forgotten wild lives. For example, when you walk your dog, chances are it will have its head down most of the time, nose sniffing the ground. This is because wild dogs needed a keen sense of smell to sniff out prey. Your dog may get its food from a dish, but it still has the ability to catch the scent of other animals.

In many ways, dogs still act like their wild ancestors. They sniff around because their ancestors used their sense of smell to find prey. They chase and retrieve because this is how wild dogs learned hunting skills. And they show affection to their pack—the human family.

When you come home from school, does your dog run to greet you? When your family goes out, does your dog howl? These actions, too, can be traced to the lives led by its wild ancestors—and the lives led today by its close relatives (wild dogs, wolves, coyotes, and jackals).

In the wild, wolves often work as a team and hunt in packs. When a dog lives with a human family, the family takes the place of the pack. Your dog runs to you when you come home because it is greeting you as a pack member. The dog worries when it is left alone, and it howls in the hope that its "pack" will hear it and answer —just as wolves do when they are separated.

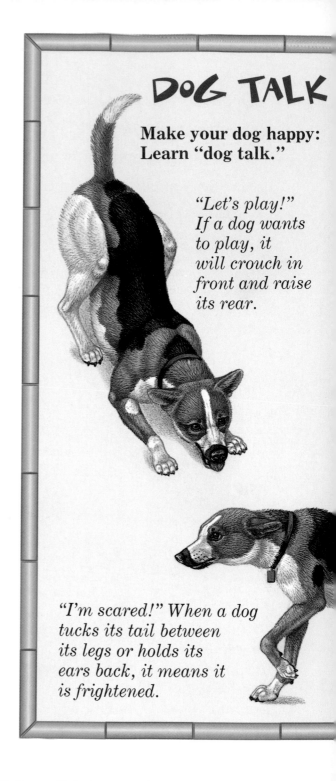

DOG TALK

Make your dog happy: Learn "dog talk."

"Let's play!" If a dog wants to play, it will crouch in front and raise its rear.

"I'm scared!" When a dog tucks its tail between its legs or holds its ears back, it means it is frightened.

Digging is also an important skill for wild dogs. They may dig to find small burrowing animals or to bury leftover food. So if your dog buries bones or hides biscuits around the house, it is just

"I'm the boss!" Stiff posture, an upright tail, and a direct stare are all signs of aggression—even if the dog's tail is wagging. Upright ears and bared teeth are stronger signs—they show that the dog is very angry.

"You're the boss!" Dogs are usually submissive with family members. That is, they give in. They show submission by crouching and holding their ears back. They may whine, too.

"I'm just a baby!" When a dog is really *submissive,* it acts like a puppy: It rolls over on its back.

reflecting its wild heritage. Even the traits that make dogs so friendly and affectionate are related to natural instincts. Watch the way your dog acts—can you spot clues to its wild life?

Simba and the Creepy Crawly

It was lunchtime in the jungle and Simba and his pals, Timon and Pumbaa, were looking for bugs to eat. They looked under logs and beneath rocks. They pawed through piles of leaves and sniffed behind ferns. But no matter where they looked, they couldn't find a single bug to munch.

"What's going on around here?" Timon asked. "I can't find a single slimy centipede or crunchy caterpillar."

"We're all out of my favorite little cream-filled bugs, too," Pumbaa sighed. His stomach growled loudly.

Simba was sniffing around the bottom of a big anthill. "That's funny," he said. "There were plenty of ants here yesterday. It looks as if someone has slurped them all up."

Just then Simba saw a long, thin trail slithering around and around the bottom of the anthill. The trail wound off into the trees. "Look at this trail," Simba called to his friends. "I think whoever made it has been eating our bugs. Let's follow the trail and see who it is."

"I hope it's not another carnivore," Timon grumbled as he climbed on Pumbaa's back. "No offense, Simba, but one of your kind around here is enough." Simba laughed. He followed the trail into the trees. Timon and Pumbaa stayed close behind.

The trail went around a large, spreading thorn bush. It wound around the trunks of tall trees and curved between tangly vines. Simba and his friends followed the trail further and further into the jungle.

"We've never gone this deep into the jungle before," Pumbaa said nervously. "I hope we can find our way back."

"It's awfully quiet and dark in here." Timon said. He whistled softly to keep his courage up.

Suddenly Simba stopped by a thicket. "Ssssh," he said. "I hear something on the other side."

Everyone listened. Hissing, slurping noises were coming from the other side of the thicket. Carefully, they peered through the branches.

On the other side they saw a fallen tree trunk. And next to it lay an enormous python. Its long brown and black splotched body was coiled in loops. Its large head swayed back and forth, and its forked tongue darted in and out as it slurped slugs off the trunk.

"A snake!" Timon exclaimed.
"They're worse than carnivores.
Always slinking here, slinking there. They
creep up on you, wanting to give you a friendly
squeeze. With that snake hanging around in the jungle I'll never
be able to enjoy my lunch again. What am I saying? I'll BE lunch!"

Luckily, the snake didn't see the three friends watching him. He
was too busy snacking on slugs. "We need to think of a plan to
make that snake leave the jungle and hunt bugs somewhere else,"
Simba said quietly.

"Maybe we can just ask him nicely to leave," Pumbaa suggested.

"Are you CRAZY?" Timon exclaimed. "Have you ever tried to
talk to a snake in the grass?"

Then Simba had an idea. "Let's disguise ourselves as bugs," he suggested. "The snake will chase us, and we can lead him out of the jungle and wherever we want him to go."

"Saaay! That might really work!" Timon agreed.

Pumbaa nodded his head, slowly. "I just hope we can run fast

enough to stay ahead of the snake," he said. "I wouldn't want to get squeezed into a corner by that guy."

They tiptoed away to find their disguises. Timon picked large leaves, and he used vines to tie the leaves onto himself, Pumbaa, and Simba. The leaves looked like big, green bug wings. Next he stuck ferns on their heads with globs of mud. The ferns looked like curly feelers. Then he spotted each of them with mud.

20

"We look like giant ladybugs!" Timon said. The others laughed. But they felt a little scared as they hurried back. The snake was still there, slurping away.

"You go first, Simba," Timon suggested.

Simba pounced over the thicket and landed beside the snake. "Buzz, buzz!" Simba shouted, whirling around as if he were a bug. The snake stared at him in amazement.

"That's the biggessssst ladybug I've ever sssseen!" he hissed. He started to crawl toward Simba. Just then Timon and Pumbaa crashed through the thicket. The snake blinked. "Three ladybugsssss," he said. "And they all look delicioussss!" He snapped at Timon.

Timon ducked away. "Run!" he shouted.

With the snake close on their heels, the three friends raced through the thicket, flapping their leaf wings and making silly buzzing noises.

"Come back! Come back!" the snake called as he slithered after them. But the threesome didn't stop or even look back.

Suddenly Simba saw a large muddy hole. "You two hide," he told Pumbaa and Timon. "I'm going to slow that snake down."

Pumbaa and Timon ducked behind a tree. Simba raced for the mud hole. The snake raced after him.

When he came to the edge of the hole, Simba jumped over it. But snakes can't jump. And this snake was going too fast to slow down. *Splash!* With a surprised hiss, the snake fell in the mud hole.

"Ummph! Ooomph!" The snake
grunted as he crawled out of the
hole. He was covered from nose
to tail with thick, sticky mud.
"How can I ssslither with this
mud all over my beautiful coils?"
the snake muttered. "But I must
have those juicy-looking ladybugs
for lunch. I can't let them ssslip away."

Dripping, slipping, and sliding, the snake started after Timon,
Simba, and Pumbaa again.

"Let's lead him toward that big thorn bush we passed at the
edge of the jungle," Timon whispered to Simba as they ran.

When they reached the thorn bush, Timon ducked beneath it.
"I'm small enough to get through this thorn bush without getting
stuck," he told his friends. "Go around and wait for me on the other
side." Simba and Pumbaa hurried off just as the snake came
slithering into view.

When Timon saw the snake, the meerkat jumped up and down. "Buzz, buzz! Over here!" he shouted. As the snake slithered after Timon, the smallest "ladybug" ducked into the thorn bush.

Pumbaa and Simba heard loud hissing and groaning sounds coming from the middle of the thorn bush as thorns pricked and

scratched the snake. Suddenly Timon burst out of the thorn bush. A moment later, the snake emerged. He was covered with thorns. Thorns were stuck in the mud on his tail. Thorns clung to the mud on his head and coils. He looked like a skinny, stretched-out bristly porcupine.

When the snake saw Timon and the others, he was furious. With a loud hiss, he started after them again. "You won't get away from —ouch!—me thissss time—ow!" he hissed. The mud made his coils stiff. The thorns scratched him. But he kept coming.

Timon jumped on Pumbaa's back. "Move it!" he shouted. Pumbaa and Timon raced away from the thorn bush with Simba at their side.

"We're almost out of the jungle!" Timon shouted. "Now what do we do?"

Pumbaa saw a tall, thin tree at the edge of the jungle overlooking the plains. He raced around the tree with Timon clinging to his back. Hissing and sputtering, the snake slithered after them. But the python was a very long snake. He met his own tail as he circled the tree. Quickly, Pumbaa ducked under the

snake's tail and circled the tree again. The snake ducked under his tail as well, and slithered around the tree after Pumbaa. Around and around the tree, Pumbaa circled, ducking under the python's tail each time. Around and around the snake went, too. Suddenly the snake jerked to a halt with a loud hiss. His coils were knotted around the tree like a long piece of rope.

Pumbaa stood panting. He and his friends stared at the snake. The snake glared back. "You are the most troublesssssome ladybugs I've ever sssseen," he hissed at them as he untangled himself. "I have mud in my coils and thorns on my nose. My beautiful long tail is in knots. I'm going ssssomewhere where bugsss hold ssstill long enough to let me eat them."

The three friends watched the python slither and bump away. Then they took off their disguises. "Wow! That was exciting!" Simba said.

"Yeah," Timon answered, "but I don't want to do it every day."

"But we still haven't had lunch," Pumbaa pointed out. "And we're still out of bugs."

Simba gave Pumbaa one of his leaf wings. "Hakuna Matata!" he said. "Munch on this, and pretend that you're crunching a giant ladybug!"

Happy Birthday, SMOKEY!

He's big and furry and always wears a ranger hat. He's appeared on posters, in cartoons, and even on a postage stamp. This world-famous superstar has a world-famous message: "Only *you* can prevent forest fires!" Yes, it's Smokey Bear—the famous mascot of forest-fire prevention in the United States. And in 1994, Smokey celebrated his 50th birthday.

The U.S. Forest Service started the Smokey Bear program in the 1940's. At that time, forest fires caused by people burned millions of acres of land. The character of a bear was chosen as the program's mascot, and Smokey first appeared on a poster in 1944.

In 1950, a fire swept through a forest in New Mexico, and a young bear with burned paws was found clinging to a tree. The cub was named

1947

PLEASE FOLKS, be **extra** careful this year!

Remember— Only **you** can PREVENT FOREST FIRES!

Smokey Bear, and he became the *living* mascot of the fire-fighting program. He lived at the National Zoo in Washington, D.C., for 26 years. When he died, he was buried in New Mexico, in Smokey Bear Historical State Park.

SMOKEY'S A·B·C's

Always break matches in two!

Be sure fires are out-cold!

Crush all smokes dead!

Please! Only you prevent forest fires

NATIONWIDE COOPERATIVE FOREST FIRE PREVENTION CAMPAIGN
SPONSORED AS A PUBLIC SERVICE BY AMERICAN BUSINESS

State Forestry Department

1963

1987

THANKS
SMOKEY
...for Helping
PREVENT FOREST FIRES

THANKS
SMOKEY

1980

SMOKEY

Only you can prevent forest fires

The character of Smokey Bear still remains the symbol of forest-fire prevention. He has been very successful. Since he first began spreading his message, the number of wildfires set by people has been cut in half.

Good job, Smokey!

This dust mite has been enormously enlarged with a scanning electron microscope. Thousands of these tiny mites live in the dust in your house.

HIDDEN WORLDS

Fierce monsters and lumpy squares . . . wormlike squiggles and weird, spiked balls . . . slimy tangles and cube-shaped rocks. You are surrounded by a world of mysterious objects! But they are too small to be seen by the naked eye. You can only see them with a special, super-powered microscope.

Ordinary microscopes are optical instruments—that is, they use light to create images. Some ordinary microscopes can magnify objects as much as 1,400 times. This may seem like a lot. But it is not enough magnification to see extremely tiny details—such as the fingerprint-like pattern on the skin of a dust mite (shown in the photo on the opposite page).

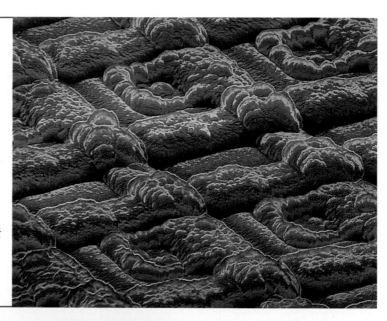

DON'T LIE DOWN!
This isn't a lumpy mattress. It's part of a computer chip that's been greatly magnified to show some of its tiny electrical pathways. Chips store information and carry out program instructions. They are the most important parts of computers—yet each chip is smaller than the tip of your finger.

PLAQUE ATTACK
Here's what happens when you don't brush your teeth after a meal. A thin, sticky film called plaque forms on your teeth. If the plaque isn't removed, bacteria in the plaque begin to attack your teeth and gums. This can lead to cavities and tooth loss. So make sure you use that toothbrush!

In order to study such tiny structures, scientists use scanning electron microscopes. These microscopes use electrons instead of light to create images. Electrons are tiny atomic particles that are part of all substances. Scanning electron microscopes can magnify objects up to 1,000,000 times! Images formed by scanning electron microscopes are black and white, and they are seen on a television screen. With the use of a computer, the images—like the ones on these pages—can be colored to highlight details.

BREAD SPREAD
This is a close-up view of mold on moist bread. The ball-shaped structure contains thousands of spores. As the spores ripen, they turn black. The ball then bursts open and the spores are released—growing into new molds.

GESUNDHEIT!
Hay fever is an allergy to pollen, which is made by flowers. When you breathe pollen into your nose, throat, and lungs, you sneeze, which helps you get rid of the pollen. This is a close-up view of ragweed pollen.

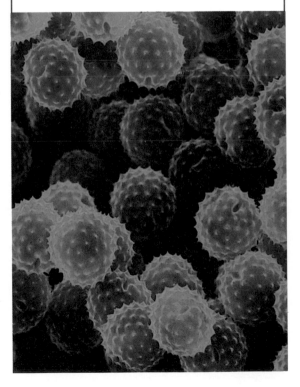

A SHEET OF TANGLES
This isn't a mess of dried spaghetti. It's a greatly magnified view of ordinary paper! Paper is made of millions of tiny fibers of cellulose, a substance in the cell walls of plants. Each fiber is about 1/20 inch long. The fibers are mixed with water, matted into a sheet, and dried to form paper.

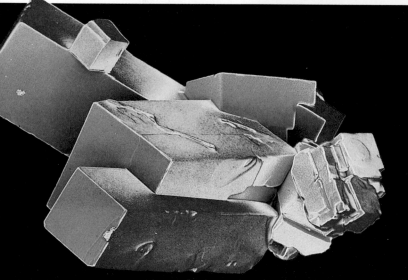

ROCKS YOU CAN EAT
These "rocks" are greatly enlarged grains of ordinary table salt. Salt consists of the chemical sodium chloride. The molecules of sodium chloride form these six-sided geometric structures, which are called crystals.

The scanning electron microscope is an important tool for scientists. They can use the microscope to find new cures for diseases. They can figure out where air pollutants came from and help clean up the air. They can design more powerful computers. In fact, scientists can use this special microscope to learn more about almost any kind of object in the hidden world around you.

SWEET SWEATS

Would you like to decorate your sweatshirts and T-shirts with your favorite desserts? To make a "sweet sweat" you will need scissors, fabric glue, different colors of felt, and small bottles of fabric paints.

Start by creating your design on paper. Cut it out and position it on the shirt. When you are pleased with the design, use the paper pattern to cut out the felt. Then paste the felt on the shirt. Be creative! (Tip: If you use a new shirt, wash it first. After the shirt is decorated, hand-wash it in cool water.)

Dandy Candy. Make a white felt cane covered with stripes of pink felt. Glue plastic gems to the cane and the shirt.

Apple Delight. Use red felt apples and green felt leaves. Draw veins on the leaves with green paint.

Ice-Cream Madness. Paint the figure in black, and add a red smile. Make two beige felt cones and two felt scoops of ice cream. Use brown paint to add cross-hatching to the cones.

Cupcake Craze. Use brown and white felt for the iced chocolate cupcakes. Cover the icing with red and white dots of paint.

Ginger Goodies. Use brown felt to make a parade of gingerbread cookies. Use orange and white paints to outline the figures and add features.

Triple Treat. Use beige felt for the cone and three "ice-creamy" colors for the scoops. Add paint sprinkles and a felt cherry.

The Princess and the Court Jester

Long ago and far away, a king, a queen, and a princess lived in a valley surrounded by mountains. Few travelers were able to find the one road that led through the mountains. But there was another reason travelers rarely came to call: A huge, scary giant lived in a cave next to the mountain road.

Princess Minnie's very best friend, Princess Clarabelle, lived in a neighboring kingdom. Once a year, Princess Minnie visited her friend. The king sent his bravest knights, Sir Donald and Sir Goofy, to escort Princess Minnie and protect her from the huge, scary giant.

36

The day before Princess Minnie's journey was like almost every other day. In the afternoon, the court jester entertained the royal family. "Your majesty, I, er, oops!" said Mickey, as he slipped on a banana peel and landed with a THUD. The king laughed. Then Mickey made a bouquet of flowers appear out of thin air. The king, the queen, and the princess applauded the jester's antics. "May I join Princess Minnie's escort party?" Mickey asked.

"Ha, ha!" laughed the king. "You, Court Jester? Will you fight the giant with laughter? Will you disarm him with magic tricks?"

Everyone, including Mickey, laughed. "Sire, I wish only to keep Princess Minnie amused," Mickey said with a bow. He looked at the princess. Her smile filled his heart with joy. The court jester was deeply in love with his princess.

"Princess?" asked the king. "Do you wish it?"

Princess Minnie's eyes shone. "Oh, yes, Father!" she said happily. The princess was secretly in love with the court jester, but she didn't dare let her love show. (Princess Minnie had read every book on the subject, and she couldn't find one single story about a princess marrying a court jester.)

The next day, Princess Minnie, Sir Donald, Sir Goofy, and the court jester set off. "What's he doing with us?" squawked Sir Donald.

"Gawrsh," said Sir Goofy, "I think the court jester is a swell guy. See?" Sir Goofy laughed as Mickey pulled an egg out of his ear.

Princess Minnie laughed. Sir Donald muttered and rode ahead.

The king's scouts met the travelers as they neared the mountains. "The giant is asleep," they reported. Quickly and quietly Princess Minnie and her party slipped through the mountain pass.

When they got to the neighboring kingdom, Princess Clarabelle rushed down the palace steps to meet them. "Minnie!" exclaimed Princess Clarabelle. The two princesses embraced. Then Princess Clarabelle said to her friend's escorts, "Welcome, all! I hope you will enjoy yourselves in my kingdom."

Princess Clarabelle's lady-in-waiting, Lady Daisy, smiled at Sir Donald. "Ah, Lady Daisy," said Sir Donald suavely, bending low and kissing her outstretched hand. "We meet again."

Sir Horace, Princess Clarabelle's bravest knight, greeted his pal Sir Goofy. "I'm experimenting with a new secret weapon. I would be glad of your help," whispered Sir Horace.

While Sir Donald and Sir Goofy visited with their friends, Mickey stayed with the princesses and entertained them.

Several days later it was time to leave. Princess Clarabelle said a tearful good-bye to Princess Minnie. Lady Daisy made Sir Donald promise to write, and Sir Horace insisted that Sir Goofy take the new secret weapon to show his king.

Unfortunately, when Princess Minnie and her escorts reached the mountain pass, the giant was awake and standing in the road.

"Stand back, Princess," Sir Donald said. "Spear chucking is my specialty!" Sir Donald chucked his spear. The giant caught the spear in midair and threw it back at Sir Donald.

"Wak!" screamed Sir Donald. He ducked as the spear sailed over his head, barely missing him.

"Time for Sir Horace's secret weapon," Sir Goofy said. He unfurled a long sheet of stretchy cloth. Sir Donald held the center while Princess Minnie and Mickey held the ends. Then Sir Goofy picked up the largest boulder he could carry. He walked toward the center and explained, "It works like a giant slingshot. When I yell 'let 'er go!' . . . yikes!"

Sir Donald let go, and Sir Goofy, still holding the boulder, flew through the air toward the giant. The giant batted him aside as if he were a pesky fly.

"Yeow!" yelled Sir Donald when Sir Goofy landed on top of him.

"Gawrsh. Sorry, Sir Donald," said Sir Goofy, getting up.

"Oh, dear!" sighed Princess Minnie. "Will we ever get home?"

"We'll think of something," said Mickey, and they all sat down to think. The giant sat down, too. They rested their chins on their fists. The giant rested his chin on his fist. Then Mickey whispered to Princess Minnie, "I have an idea. Wait here."

Mickey stood up. The giant stood up. Mickey shook his head

from side to side. The giant shook his head from side to side. Mickey said, "Hiya!" The giant shouted, "Hiya!"

Mickey stood on one foot and flapped his arms.

The giant stood on one foot and flapped his arms.

Mickey tiptoed in a circle with his arms over his head like a little ballerina.

The giant tiptoed in a circle with his arms over his head like a little ballerina.

Whatever Mickey did, the giant did too.

"It's a giant game of Simon, I mean, Mickey Says!" said the amazed princess.

Mickey's game with the giant continued. Mickey hopped this way. The giant hopped this way. Mickey skipped that way. The giant skipped that way. Then Mickey hopped and skipped past the giant, through the mountain pass and into the giant's cave. The giant hopped and skipped right behind him. When Mickey and the giant were out of sight, the others hurried through the pass and made their way home.

Princess Minnie watched and waited and waited and watched for Mickey's return. Hours turned into days without a sign of Mickey.

The king and queen were
concerned, but Princess Minnie
was heartbroken. In her grief,
she confessed to her parents that
she loved the court jester with
all her heart. The queen said,
"The court jester has proven

himself as brave as any knight. If he returns to the castle we shall
make him a knight, and then you and he may marry."

"Thank you, Mother," cried Princess Minnie. Just then the castle
began to shake, and an awful booming sound was heard in the
distance. The royal family rushed out onto the balcony. The
booming grew louder and clearer, "Hiya! HIYA! Hellooo!
HELLOOO!"

Then suddenly the giant was standing before them. But the royal family was not afraid. In fact, the king and queen laughed, and Princess Minnie cried happy tears. There was Mickey sitting on the giant's shoulder, waving his jester's wand.

The giant put Mickey down on the ground. Then the giant said, "Say, Mickey, where does the king sit?"

"I don't know," Mickey answered, playing the straight man. "Where does the king sit?"

The giant smiled and delivered the punchline, "Anywhere he wants to!"

"Bravo!" shouted the king, applauding his favorite joke.

"Oh, Mickey," sighed Princess Minnie.

Then the king commanded, "Court Jester, kneel!"

"Y-y-yes, Your Majesty," Mickey said, kneeling.

"For acts of bravery, tricks of magic, and jocular jokery, I dub thee Sir Mickey. Arise, Sir Knight!" the king said.

"Oh, Mickey, I mean, Sir Mickey!" exclaimed Princess Minnie.

"Gee, Princess, now that I'm a knight, will you . . ." he asked.

"Yes!" cried Princess Minnie before he could even finish the question.

There's never been a story about a princess marrying a court jester . . . until now.

MYSTERY OF THE VANISHING FROGS

On cool spring nights, a croaking chorus of frogs is a familiar sound around woodland ponds. Yet in many places, this froggy melody has mysteriously disappeared. When scientists began to investigate, they found something alarming: All over the world, the number of frogs is declining. And scientists aren't sure why.

Frogs are one of the oldest kinds of living things. They first appeared on Earth about 180 million years ago. There are several thousand species (kinds) of frogs and their close relatives, toads. And they live in nearly every part of the world.

Frogs are amphibians—they spend part of their lives in water and part on land. Scientists think that amphibians are a link between fish and land animals. They believe that amphibians developed from fish, and that land animals developed from early amphibians. The life cycle of a frog mirrors this change from water to land. Most frogs lay their eggs in water. When the eggs hatch, tiny tadpoles swim out. A tadpole looks like a fish, with a tail for swimming and gills for breathing in water. But in time, the tadpole changes into a frog with four legs for hopping on land and lungs for breathing air.

Opposite page: Red-eyed tree frogs of Central America, and the dumpy tree frog of Australia.
This page: Tomato frogs of Madagascar, a yellow dart-poison frog of tropical America, and the bullfrog of North America.

Once Upon a Frog

Once upon a time, a prince was turned into an ugly frog. Only a kiss from a princess would turn him back into a man. This well-known fairy tale is just one of the many stories, legends, and beliefs concerning frogs.

In many cultures, for example, frogs have been associated with rain—probably because frogs need moisture and often appear after a rain. Some people thought that frogs had the power to make it rain. Some even believed that frogs fell from the sky with rain.

In the 1800's, the American writer Mark Twain wrote about a frog-jumping contest in Calaveras County, California. Today, that contest is re-enacted every year. Also, one of the best-known book characters is Mr. Toad of Wind in the Willows. *And one of the most popular characters on TV is a frog puppet named Kermit!*

Most adult frogs have moist, smooth skin, bulging eyes, four legs, and no tail. But this basic body plan is just a starting point. Frogs have unique features that make them among the most varied animals on Earth. In size alone, they range from tiny species just ½ inch long to the huge Goliath frog of West Africa, which is nearly 1 foot long.

Many frogs are colored to blend with their surroundings. This helps them to sneak up on prey, and to stay hidden from enemies. Frogs that live high in the trees are often bright green, while those that live in forests may be shades of green, brown, or black. Other frogs are brightly colored. They can't hide so easily, but their bright colors serve a purpose. These frogs usually have skin glands that secrete poisons. Enemies quickly learn to leave these colorful frogs alone because they aren't very tasty!

Frogs spend most of their time looking for food—or waiting for food to pass by. Most frogs eat insects, which they catch with their long, sticky tongues. But some big frogs can eat mice and

To attract a mate, this barking tree frog puffs out the sac under his chin to make his voice louder.

Most frogs, such as this European tree frog, capture prey by flicking out their long, sticky tongues.

lizards, and even other frogs. Frogs also need water, which they absorb through their skin. Thus, even frogs that don't live in ponds need a moist environment to survive.

Frogs have powerful hind legs and are terrific jumpers.

But because they remain perfectly still much of the time and jump away quickly when danger comes near, it is easier to hear a frog than see one. Peeps and croaks are common frog calls. However, some frogs sound like tinkling bells, flutes, and even barking dogs.

Today these amazing creatures are in danger. In ponds that were once filled with chirping, croaking amphibians, there are few or none to be found. Toads, salamanders, and other amphibians seem to be vanishing, too. And the problem is worldwide. In fact, at a special conference held in 1990, sixteen countries on five

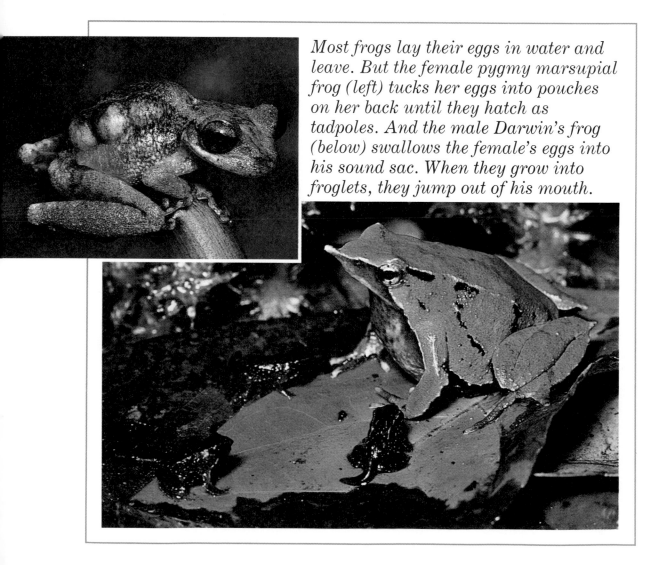

Most frogs lay their eggs in water and leave. But the female pygmy marsupial frog (left) tucks her eggs into pouches on her back until they hatch as tadpoles. And the male Darwin's frog (below) swallows the female's eggs into his sound sac. When they grow into froglets, they jump out of his mouth.

continents reported big drops in the population of amphibians. Why are these animals disappearing? Scientists don't have the answers yet, but they think that environmental problems might be a reason.

Frogs have thin skins that absorb chemicals, making them sensitive to pollution. So acid rain—which is caused by pollution from factories and cars —may be to blame.

Scientists think that an even stronger possibility is the increase in ultraviolet rays from the sun. Normally, Earth is protected from such rays by a layer of gas in the atmosphere called the ozone layer. But pollution has made the ozone layer thinner, so more ultraviolet rays get through. In 1994, scientists found that fewer frogs' eggs hatch when they are exposed to one kind of ultraviolet radiation.

Scientists are still looking for answers. Hopefully they will find them. We can't risk losing frogs, one of the oldest and most fascinating of Earth's creatures.

A Froggy Medicine Chest

Frogs were once thought to have healing powers. Some people believed that placing a young frog in a patient's mouth could cure a cough. Others rubbed live frogs on freckles to remove them. Of course, it is unlikely that any of this worked.

But for centuries, people living in rain forests have used chemicals from frogs as medicine. And today, scientists are discovering that the chemicals in the skin glands of many frogs may indeed be an important source of drugs. For instance, from chemicals found in the African clawed frog, scientists have developed an antibiotic that helps fight skin diseases. And from an Ecuadorian frog, researchers have developed a strong painkiller.

Three brightly colored balls circle swiftly in the air above your head. You add a fourth, then a fifth—and they never fall to the ground. Is it a magic trick? No, it's juggling!

Juggling is the art of tossing and catching objects in the air. Almost anyone can do it, but it takes LOTS of practice. (Some top jugglers have been known to practice ten hours a day!) You can learn to juggle many different things—balls, oranges, hoops, rings, and clubs. So why not try *your* hand at juggling?

There are several basic tossing patterns. One of the easiest is the cascade. With the cascade, the objects are popped from hand to hand in a pattern that looks something like a figure-eight turned on its side. A more difficult technique is the shower, in which the objects are kept moving in a circle. Some jugglers use still another method. Rather than tossing the objects from hand to hand, they juggle half the objects with one hand and half with the other.

Here are a few juggling hints: To add more objects, toss higher—the higher an object goes, the longer it takes to come down.

Hoops are easier to juggle than balls because you can catch a hoop by sticking your arm through the middle. Clubs are harder to juggle than balls because they have to be caught by the proper end. Begin with lightweight objects such as the juggling scarves shown above—they fall very slowly.

If you would like to get started in juggling, just turn the page. And remember: Practice makes perfect.

THE ACTION
Toss a ball straight up into the air. Keep your wrists stiff. Try not to move your upper arm.

THE POP
Toss a ball from your right hand to the X spot above your left hand. Catch the ball in your left hand. Now "pop" it back the other way.

THE STANCE
Stand with your feet 1 foot apart, and your hands palms up. Imagine two X's in the air above your hands at eye level. As you juggle, watch the "X spots," not your hands.

TWO-BALL POP
Hold a ball in each hand. Pop ball 1 up to the opposite X spot. When it reaches the X spot, pop ball 2 up to its opposite X spot.

THREE-BALL JUGGLE
Start with two balls in one hand and one in the other. Proceed as if you are going to pop two balls—but before you catch ball 2, pop ball 3.

THE CARPET IS MISSING!

It was a slow day in Agrabah. Abu, the monkey who was
Aladdin's pal, and the magic carpet were flying low over the city
looking for something to do. As they cruised over the marketplace,
Abu spotted a caravan.

Now, this was no ordinary caravan. It belonged to Karakter,
the greedy, unscrupulous ringleader of a band of treasure thieves.

Looking closer, Abu spotted a treasure chest waiting to be
loaded on a camel. It was totally irresistible! "Oh boy!" he
squealed. Then they swooped down toward the caravan.

As usual, it now became the carpet's job to stop Abu. The carpet tried to hold Abu back, but the monkey slipped free. Then, just as Abu was pocketing a fistful of jewels, the carpet tugged at his elbow again. Abu jerked his arm away and knocked the carpet right into the treasure chest!

Suddenly one of Karakter's guards slammed the lid of the chest shut, locking the carpet inside. Then, seeing Abu, the guard yelled, "Get away from here, monkey!"

Abu dashed out of the way, but he knew that the caravan was about to leave. And the carpet was trapped in the treasure chest! He had to get help! So away he ran to get Aladdin.

While Abu was racing back to the palace, Karakter and his bullies quickly loaded up their camels. "Hurry up, you idiots!" screamed Karakter. "If we can get to the Allamine Oasis before anyone else, the world's biggest treasure will be mine!"

Back in Agrabah, a breathless Abu found Aladdin and started chattering and gesturing wildly.

"Whoa! Slow down, Abu," said Aladdin. "What's wrong?"

After Abu had dramatically acted out the whole scene that had occurred with the magic carpet, and the treasure chest, and the guards with swords, Aladdin jumped up, ready to take off after the caravan. "Let's go, Abu! We've got to find that caravan!"

"I'm going with you," said Jasmine.

"This could be dangerous, Jasmine," warned Aladdin. "No telling what kind of thugs have kidnapped the carpet. I wish the Genie hadn't gone off in search of pogs, whatever they are."

"You'll need help," said Jasmine. "Somebody will have to find the carpet while you're fighting off thugs."

At that moment Iago flew down to see what all the ruckus was about. "I tell ya, it's getting harder and harder to take a nice quiet nap around here," he complained. "I could become extremely cranky if I don't get enough sleep, ya know."

"Iago, the carpet's been kidnapped by a caravan!" Jasmine explained. "We could use your help."

"Good riddance to that piece of fuzz!" squawked Iago.

Abu couldn't take it anymore. He scooted up to Iago and chattered loudly in his ear, grabbing him by the neck.

"Hold on, Abu," said Aladdin, peeling his buddy away from Iago. "The longer we stay here arguing, the farther away that caravan gets. We've got to get going."

"Say, Iago," Jasmine said soothingly, "according to Abu, the carpet is trapped inside a treasure chest. If you flew ahead and

delayed the caravan so we could catch up, Aladdin would arrange a nice reward for you. Right, Aladdin?"

Aladdin blinked in surprise at Jasmine. "Uh, right. Sure. There'll be a reward in it for Iago."

The next thing he knew, Iago was flying after the caravan. "I can't believe I'm doing this. And for that fuzz blanket."

A few hours later, the caravan stopped for the night. While the guards broke out the tents and unloaded the camels, Karakter went down the line to check on the treasure chest that held the carpet captive. Even though he was after bigger booty, he wasn't about to lose the treasure he already had.

"Well, well," said Karakter, opening the chest, "what have we here? I thought this chest held treasure, not rugs."

He reached for the carpet just as the little guy started to zip away. Too late! The carpet tugged and tugged, but Karakter tightened his grip, pulling off one of the carpet's tassels. Like a wounded puppy, the carpet curled up and played dead, hoping this mean man would leave him alone.

But Karakter had figured out that this was a magic carpet, with a lot of power in its golden tassels. Quickly, Karakter snipped them all off! "Heh, heh!" he chortled. "I'll string all my camels together and use these tassels to fly the whole kit and caboodle to the oasis. We'll beat everyone to the treasure!"

Poor carpet! He couldn't fly without his tassels. Now he was just an ordinary rug—but one with feelings.

Just then Iago zoomed right down on top of the carpet, who was rolled up next to Karakter. "Wow!" said Iago, looking straight into

Karakter's face. "Lucky shot!
So where's the treasure, bully boy?"

"What?" Karakter boomed.

Iago ruffled his wings, trying to stand tall. "I'm here to retrieve this little fuzz blanket and collect my reward. What did you do with his little gold tassels?"

"Those tassels are going to get me the biggest treasure this side of the Nile."

Iago was pleased. "Count me in," he said.

"Forget it, featherbrain!" said Karakter. He shoved Iago into an urn and stuffed the carpet in after him. Clutching the tassels, he began to hook the caravan together.

Just then Aladdin, Abu, and Jasmine arrived. But several armed thugs stood between them and the caravan.

"Uh-oh! Stay back, Jasmine!" shouted Aladdin.

Aladdin galloped off toward a nearby dune. He wanted the bullies to follow him and leave Jasmine alone.

It worked! While Aladdin led the thugs away, Jasmine aimed for a tent where she could hear some muffled squawking. That had to be Iago!

Jasmine snuck up and peeked inside the tent. Gold platters and pitchers and other treasures were scattered all around. Then, off in a corner, she spotted a gold urn with the end of a carpet sticking out. Iago's squawks came from the urn.

It took quite a bit of pulling, but Jasmine managed to free the carpet. Then she turned the urn upside down and shook it. *Thump!*

Out came Iago, spitting and sputtering. "I can't believe it!" he wailed. "Why do I always end up in little, tiny spaces? At least this time I wasn't stuck with Jafar!"

"Iago!" whispered Jasmine. "What has happened to the carpet? All his tassels are missing."

"They are? Oh, yeah, they are," said the parrot. "Some guy said something about using them to get a huge treasure. Then he stuffed me in that urn. *Ptooi!* I hate when that happens!"

"Iago," Jasmine said urgently, "you've got to get those tassels back! Please! Hurry!"

"Whoa!" Iago complained. "You women get so touchy about fuzzy things. All right, all right. I'm off on a tassel trip."

Meanwhile, Aladdin had lost Karakter's guards and was heading back to the caravan. All of a sudden, he ran into Iago carrying the carpet's gold tassels in his beak. "Iago! Where's the carpet? Where's Jasmine?"

The parrot spit the tassels out into Aladdin's hands. "They're in one of these tents, but I can't remember which one."

Grabbing Iago by the wing, Aladdin quickly went from tent to tent until he found Jasmine.

"Oh, Aladdin!" she cried, "I'm so glad it's you. Quick! Give me those tassels!" Pulling the ribbons from her hair, Jasmine used them to tie the tassels back onto the corners of the carpet.

Just as she was fastening the last tassel to the carpet, Karakter burst in, waving his sword in the air. "Those are *my* tassels!" he screamed.

"But it's *my* magic carpet!" Aladdin shouted. "Carpet, take us back to Agrabah! And step on it!"

The carpet veered crazily as Karakter took a swing at the tassels. And then they were all soaring through the sky!

Aladdin looked back at the caravan. Karakter was standing beside a camel, shaking his fist. "That was close," he said.

"Ya know," chirped Iago, "it's too bad. I keep getting stuffed into small spaces, and all I ever come up with is a mouthful of sand."

Aladdin and Jasmine laughed. Abu just muttered under his breath. Another treasure gone—all because of a greedy parrot!

PEOPLE WORDS

SANDWICH

About two hundred years ago in Britain, the Earl of Sandwich was playing cards with friends. Not wanting to leave the table for a meal, he asked his servant to bring a slice of meat between two pieces of bread. This style of food soon became known as a **sandwich,** and the Earl became an *eponym*—a person for whom something is named.

The French have also given us many "people words." In 1859, for example, Jules Léotard

LEOTARD

GARGANTUAN

POMPADOUR

dazzled French audiences by soaring through the air on the first flying trapeze. His tight-fitting costume became known as a **leotard.**

During the 1500's, a well-known French author wrote about a giant that he called Gargantua, to poke fun at the greedy nobles of his day. Gargantua was so huge that the horse he rode was as big as six elephants! Today the word **gargantuan** is used to describe something that is truly enormous.

During the mid-1700's, Madame Pompadour was a favorite of King Louis XV of France. A beautiful woman, she wore her hair swept up from her forehead. That style, called a **pompadour,** has been popular several times since her day.

71

A PEEK INTO SPACE

The moon, the stars, and the planets—these are just a few of the billions of objects in outer space. To peek at these far-away objects, you need to use a telescope. A telescope makes distant things seem closer and clearer.

Thanks to telescopes, people saw a spectacular collision in space in 1994. In July, 21 mountain-sized pieces of a broken comet slammed into the atmosphere of the planet Jupiter. There were huge explosions as the pieces were destroyed, and enormous fireballs flew into space. And Jupiter's atmosphere was pockmarked with large dark scars.

Bright spots show where pieces of a comet crashed into Jupiter's atmosphere.

Most telescopes that watched the heavenly collision were on Earth. However, some telescopes were in space. One of these was the Hubble Space Telescope. Hubble was launched in 1990, but scientists discovered that its main mirror wasn't working properly. As a result, the telescope was "nearsighted"—it couldn't see clearly, and the photographs it took were fuzzy.

In 1993, astronauts aboard the space shuttle *Endeavour* flew to Hubble. During a series of daring space walks, they repaired the telescope. They added many new parts, including a giant "contact lens" that corrected its blurry vision. They also installed a new camera. Now Hubble takes sharp, clear photographs, and scientists can see farther into space than ever before.

Scientists on Earth can point Hubble at different objects in space. Hubble photographs the objects and sends the pictures by radio to computers on Earth. And Hubble has discovered

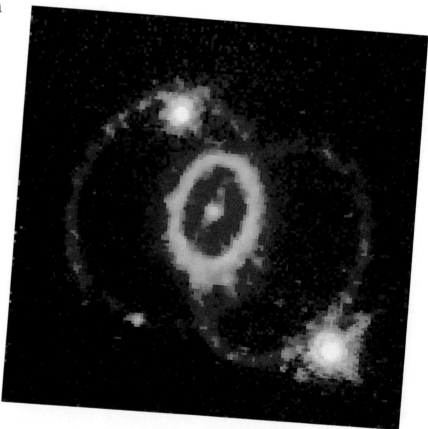

Hubble photographed strange rings of glowing gas around an exploded star.

amazing things. For example, the sharp-eyed telescope looked at a star that had recently exploded. It found two huge, mysterious rings of glowing gas around the star's remains. No one had ever seen these strange "hula hoops" in space before!

Hubble also took the first photograph of a black hole. A black hole is a very, very dense space object. Because it is so dense, its gravity is very powerful—so powerful that nothing can escape from it, not even light. The Hubble photograph showed glowing gases being sucked into the black hole.

Pictures from Hubble and other telescopes may help scientists find answers to some fascinating questions: How old is the universe? Are there planets around other stars? Is there life elsewhere in the universe?

Left: The "nearsighted" Hubble took this fuzzy picture of a galaxy. Right: With its new "contact lens," the repaired Hubble photographed the same galaxy—and the image was much sharper.

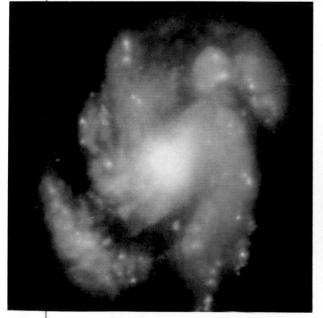 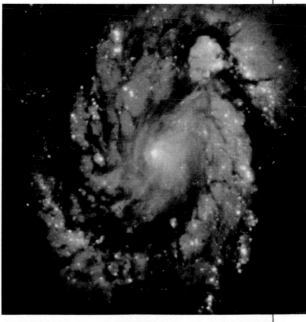

Man on the moon: Astronaut Buzz Aldrin poses for a photo.

Footprints on the Moon

In 1994, people celebrated the 25th anniversary of the first human visit to the moon.

On July 20, 1969, astronauts Neil Armstrong and Edwin "Buzz" Aldrin landed their special lunar spacecraft on the dusty, rocky surface of the moon. They put on special clothing that would protect them, and they opened the door of their vehicle. Then, as millions of people on Earth watched the extraordinary event on television, Armstrong made the first human footprint on the moon. And he said, "That's one small step for a man, one giant leap for mankind."

The astronauts took many photographs and collected soil and rocks to bring back to Earth.

BLAST OFF!

The sun and everything that orbits around it form a family called the solar system. Our planet, Earth, is part of the solar system. Some members of the sun's family—such as the nine planets—are quite large. But there are also thousands of smaller objects. Let's blast off into outer space and see what we can find. The names of 13 members of our solar system are listed below, in the left column. Match each name to its description, in the right column.

1. Asteroids   **a.** The planet nearest the sun
2. Comet   **b.** Astronauts have walked on it
3. Earth   **c.** The largest and heaviest planet
4. Jupiter   **d.** Tiny planets
5. Mars   **e.** The last planet discovered
6. Mercury   **f.** It is known as the "Red Planet"
7. Meteor   **g.** It has a long, glowing tail
8. Moon   **h.** It is also called a shooting star
9. Neptune   **i.** Beautiful icy rings circle it
10. Pluto   **j.** It is named for the Roman god of the sea
11. Saturn   **k.** The planet closest to Earth
12. Uranus   **l.** The only known planet with living things
13. Venus   **m.** It takes 84 years to orbit the sun

ANSWERS:
1,d; 2,g; 3,l; 4,c; 5,f; 6,a; 7,h; 8,b; 9,j; 10,e; 11,i; 12,m; 13,k

The names of all the objects are hidden in this puzzle. Try to find them. Read forward, backward, up, down, and diagonally.

J	V	E	N	U	S	O	U	S	I
U	O	T	U	L	P	R	D	S	B
P	F	P	C	R	A	I	J	R	D
I	H	M	X	N	O	S	K	O	W
T	M	L	U	R	P	F	B	E	T
E	A	S	E	A	R	T	H	T	T
R	R	T	E	N	U	T	P	E	N
C	S	A	T	U	R	N	M	M	S
A	M	O	O	N	P	O	U	Y	E
R	U	M	E	R	C	U	R	Y	O

Snow White and the Seven Princes

One day, not long after Snow White had left the Seven Dwarfs'
cottage to marry her prince, the dwarfs received a note from her.

"Listen, men!" Doc said. "The princess is coming to key us, I
mean, coming to see us!"

"Harumph!" Grumpy grumbled. "It's about time. Wimmen!
They find their princes and just fergit about everybody else!"

"But she hasn't forgotten us!" Happy laughed. "Look, it says
she's coming for dinner."

"Then she's fergitten' we don't cook," Grumpy told him.

"No," Doc said, "she's just expecting us to boo our dest, I mean do our best." He squared his shoulders. "Men, the princess is used to princely behavior now. If we're going to have a visit fit for the princess, we've got to behave like princes ourselves."

"But how?" Bashful asked, looking down at the ground.

"Make tea, for example, I mean, take me," Doc said. "Why, I'm going to do my best to speak just like a prince."

Happy laughed. "I'll try not to laugh so much. I'm sure princes don't laugh very often." He tried to frown, but it came out a smile.

Sleepy stretched and yawned. "I'll try to stay awake through the dinner," he said as he dozed off.

Grumpy snorted. "He'll need a bell to keep him awake."

Dopey ran and took a bell out from behind a chair. He put a loop of rope around it, then placed it around Sleepy's neck. When he nudged Sleepy, the bell clanged, and Sleepy jumped to alertness.

"Good work, Dopey!" Doc said, pleased that he hadn't mixed up any words. Concentrating very hard, he said, "Noo's hext, I mean, who's next?"

"I'll wear a nose mitten," Sneezy said. "That way, I won't smell anything that will make me sneeze."

Doc nodded, but decided not to take any more chances by saying a full sentence. "Dopey?"

Dopey took a carved wooden whistle from the organ and held it to his mouth. Soon he was whistling a cheery tune.

Slowly and quietly, Bashful added, "I'll try to talk more to the princess," he said.

"Humph!" Grumpy said. "I see none of you thought of the most important things!" When they all looked curious enough, he said, "Hand-washing and flower-gathering. Those are my departments now! I'll have the cleanest hands and the best flowers at the table for dinner—and nobody better try to sneak a dirty hand past me!"

"Men," said Doc, "I hereby announce the start of the Program of Princely Behavior!"

The dwarfs clapped happily.

The days went by quickly, and soon it was time for the princess's visit. When Snow White stepped out of her coach, she was surprised to see that the water trough was empty—and all the dwarfs were dripping wet!

"Good evening, Princess!" Doc said with a bow. He was going to add, "Welcome back to our home," but he was too afraid that he'd mix up his words.

"Why, good evening, Doc," said Snow White. "My goodness, how did you all get so wet?"

Doc didn't answer. Instead, Bashful explained in a loud voice, "Grumpy wanted to make sure that we all washed our hands, Princess. So he dunked us one by one."

"My goodness, Bashful," said Snow White, "you're not so bashful anymore."

Bashful started to blush and turn away, but he made himself stop. "Thank you, Princess. We're all so glad you could come. Why, just today, on the way home from the mine . . ."

As Bashful kept talking, Grumpy ran to the front door of the cottage and picked up two big bunches of flowers. "Wait till you come inside! I picked every durn flower in the forest!"

"Every durn one," agreed a voice Snow White didn't recognize. She peeked behind Grumpy as the dwarfs hurried inside.

"Sneezy? Is that you?" She could barely see his face behind the large blue mitten he was putting on his nose.

"See, Princess," he answered in a muffled voice. "Now I won't sneeze anymore. Just look," he added, "all these flowers around and not one sneeze out of me!"

"Oh, my goodness!" Snow White said. Almost every table, bench, chair, and stair had flowers on it.

"Grumpy's been picking them for days," Bashful told her.

84

Then Snow White heard a bell. Sleepy came over and smiled at her. He started to doze, but as his head dropped, the bell clanged.

"Hello, Princess," he said, jumping awake.

"Hello, Slee—" Snow White started to say, but just then Dopey came up, whistling merrily.

"Why, Dopey, what a lovely whistle! Did you carve that?"

"He sure did," Bashful told her. Sleepy's bell clanged again, and the dwarfs' shoes squished as they walked.

My, thought Snow White, it is noisier here than I remember. Sleepy's clanging, Dopey's whistling, and everyone's shoes squishing made it hard to talk.

"How nice!" Snow White shouted over the whistling, clanging, and squishing. Then she spotted Happy. "Why, what's wrong?"

Happy brushed his tears away with his sleeve. It was so hard not to laugh that he had to think unhappy thoughts that made him cry. Just now, he was remembering the sad day when he and the dwarfs found Snow White asleep under the wicked queen's spell. "Nothing, Princess," he sniffled.

"But you're always so . . . happy," Snow White said.

Happy just sniffled louder. But his sniffles were soon drowned out by the squishing, clanging, and whistling.

Snow White frowned. Doc would know what was wrong. She

turned to the other dwarfs. "Now, where is Doc? I would like to talk to him."

Doc backed away behind the others and pushed Bashful forward. "Could *I* talk to you, Princess? How was your ride through the forest? Are the seven falls still falling?"

"Why, yes," Snow White answered. She couldn't believe her ears. Bashful asking questions? "Well," she said aloud, "I guess we ought to sit down. What did you make for dinner?"

Suddenly the squishing, clanging, whistling, and sniffling stopped. The dwarfs looked at each other.

"Dake for minner?" Doc said before he could stop himself.

Bashful blushed. Happy laughed. Sleepy dozed off in a corner. And Sneezy put a finger under his nose and nose mitten.

"Oh, no!" Grumpy yelled.

"AAAHHH-CHOOO!!!" With one sneeze, Sneezy blew the mitten off his nose and most of the petals off the flowers. When the petals had settled, he looked sadly at the other dwarfs. "Sorry, men," he said. "I guess I'll never be very princely after all."

"Why, Sneezy, what are you talking about?" Snow White looked around at all the dwarfs. "Why have you all been acting so odd?"

Doc came forward slowly. "It was my idea, Princess." He tried to keep his words as proper as possible. "We wanted to lee bike princes, I mean, be like princes for you. Like what you're used to now." He stared at his feet. "Princes who don't mix up their words," he added sadly.

"Or laugh too much." Happy chuckled.

"Or have dirty hands. Or be too bashful. Or sneeze too loudly. Or be so sleepy," the others said. Dopey whistled a short sad tune.

"Oh, my goodness!" Snow White said. "Oh, you are such good friends! To go to all that trouble . . ." To the dwarfs' surprise, Snow White knelt down and gave each of them a hug. "But don't you understand? I like each of you for the special thing that makes you different. Why, Sneezy, I like your sneezes. They make me laugh. And Happy, when *you* laugh, I want to laugh with you! Oh, all of you!" she said. "You are princes to me just the way you are!"

"Well, good," Grumpy snapped, " 'cause I'm not pickin' any more flowers! I got chased by a swarm of bees today!"

Snow White smiled as Sneezy ah-chooed again. Then, as Sleepy dozed and Doc chatted, as Happy laughed and Grumpy grumped, as Bashful smiled shyly and Dopey played a merry tune, Snow White made a stew fit for seven princes—and shared it with her friends.

NUDIBRANCHS. *Sometimes called sea slugs, nudibranchs are relatives of snails—but without protective shells. Fingerlike projections on the back are used to take oxygen into the body. Tentacles on the head gather information about the surroundings.*

CHRISTMAS-TREE WORMS. *These creatures may look like delicate snow-covered Christmas trees, but they are really underwater worms. The white feathery gills that circle the upper part of each worm's body are used to breathe and to gather food from the water.*

UNDERWATER SURPRISES

Diving into the sea is like traveling to another world. But many of the things in this underwater kingdom aren't what they seem. Prepare to be surprised when objects that look like feathery flowers, blobs of jelly, little bottles, and spiny pincushions turn out

PENCIL SEA URCHINS. *Thick spines cover the pencil urchin's body. At one time, people used these spines as blackboard chalk! Like other sea urchins —which resemble pincushions or underwater hedgehogs— pencil urchins use their spines to move over the ocean bottom.*

SEA VASES. *The sea vase, a species of sea squirt, has a see-through body. One end of its body is attached to a rock or perhaps a clam shell. At the other end are two openings. When something disturbs the little creature, it squirts water out of the openings.*

to be living creatures—just like the animals shown here! These amazing critters—Christmas-tree worms, nudibranchs, sea vases, and sea urchins—live in shallow waters. Finding them may not be easy. But if you look closely at rocks and wharf piles, you just might spot a few. You must keep still, though, or the creatures will quickly disappear into their sand-covered homes.

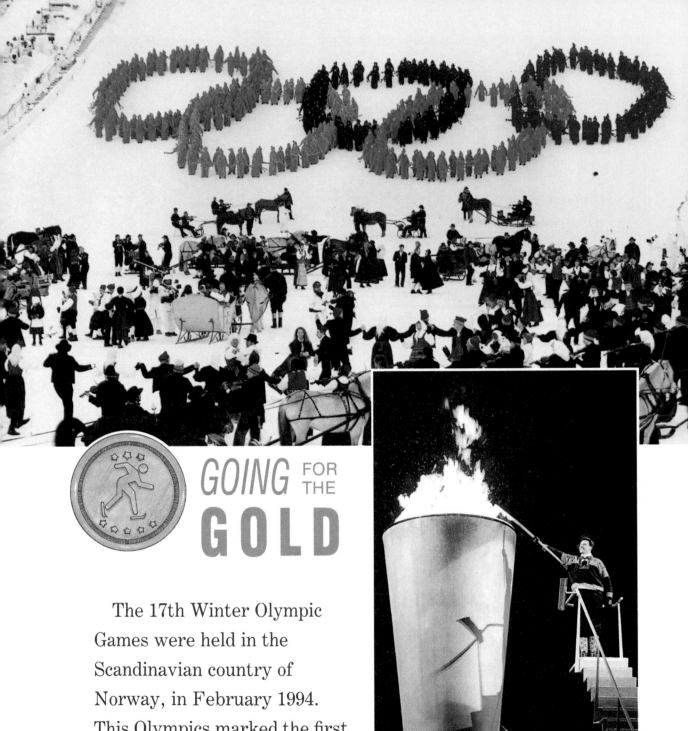

GOING FOR THE GOLD

The opening ceremonies: Four hundred children form the Olympic symbol, and Norway's Crown Prince lights the Olympic flame.

The 17th Winter Olympic Games were held in the Scandinavian country of Norway, in February 1994. This Olympics marked the first time that the Winter Games weren't followed by the Summer Games later in the year. The Games will now follow separate four-year schedules. The 1996 Summer Games will take place in Atlanta, Georgia. And the 1998 Winter Games will be held in Nagano, Japan.

The official site of the 1994 Games was the small, charming town of Lillehammer. That was also where the enchanting opening ceremonies were held. As snowflakes drifted down upon Lillehammer, 400 Norwegian children formed the five-ring symbol of the Olympics. Dancers dressed as elves popped out of the snowbanks. Sleighs pulled by horses and reindeer circled the stadium. And in a spectacular climax to the ceremonies, a Norwegian ski jumper, holding high the Olympic torch, whooshed safely down a steep hill. Norway's Crown Prince Haakon Magnus then took the torch and set the Olympic flame ablaze. The Games had begun!

The Olympic Mascots

Hakon and Kristin, figures of a Norwegian boy and girl, were the mascots of the Winter Games. They were named after real people. Hakon grew up to become king of Norway from 1217 to 1263. Kristin was his aunt. She married the leader of his rivals, which allowed Norway to become unified under Hakon's rule.

Hakon and Kristin

Nearly 2,000 athletes from 66 nations competed in 61 events. Norway won the most medals—26, including 10 golds. The United States came in fifth—with 13 medals, including 6 golds. The shining performances of a few of the winners are described here.

• One of the most popular events of any Winter Olympics is the women's figure-skating competition. Sixteen-year-old world champion Oksana Baiul of Ukraine dazzled audiences with an engaging and artistic performance. Nancy Kerrigan of the United States also skated beautifully. But when the numbers from the short and long programs were added up, Oksana Baiul had won the gold medal by the slimmest of margins. Nancy Kerrigan settled for the silver, and Chen Lu of China took the bronze.

• Tommy Moe of Alaska did something that no American skier had ever done before—he won two alpine skiing medals at one Olympics. Moe sped to the gold medal in the downhill event, beating the Norwegian favorite, Kjetil Andre Aamodt, by only half a second. He then went on to win the silver medal in the super giant slalom on—of all days—his 24th birthday!

Oksana Baiul, Ukraine, figure skating.

*Above: Tommy Moe, U.S.,
alpine skiing. Right: Dan
Jansen, U.S., speed skating.*

• American Dan Jansen
was speed skating's top
male sprinter, but he had
never won an Olympic gold.
And in 1994's 500-meter
event, he finished eighth.
But in the 1,000-meter
event, he set a world
record. Dan Jansen won the
gold and finally had his
Olympic triumph.

THE JOKES ON YOU!

What do you say to your friend if he has an egg on his head?

The yolk's on you!

How do you know if there's an elephant under your bed?

When your nose touches the ceiling!

What did the baby porcupine say to the cactus?

"Is that you, Mom?"

How can you make a witch scratch?

Take away the "w"!

What did one eye say to the other eye?

Just between you and me, something smells!

What kind of mistakes do ghosts make?

Boo-boos!